MW01601332

Amazon Echo User Guide

What to Know about Your Amazon Echo, How to Use it & Get the Most out of Your Echo

2nd Edition

Copyright 2015 by Marc Lumbell - All rights reserved.

Hello, Friend!

We enjoy books as much as you do. We love to share our upcoming projects, special deals, and FREE Gifts with you! Please take a minute and accept our invitation - IT only takes a minute to join our Special VIP Book Club at

tiny.cc/echo-bonus and start getting your special access - TODAY!

Your FREE Membership entitles you to many benefits:

- A Wealth of Free Reading Samples

- Notifications about Free and Discounted Books

- Special Early-Bird Alerts About New Titles

- Bonus Video Content

- Members-Only Reading Guides

- Special Reports

- *and even more* FREE Bonuses!

So, join the club at tiny.cc/echo-bonus and then sit back, open your Kindle reader, relax, and enjoy the show! And - don't forget - at the end of this book, you'll also find a FREE Special Bonus. This extra content is our special "thank you" to you - our valued readers!

Table Of Contents

Introduction...5

Chapter 1 – Who Should Consider Buying an Amazon Echo?7

Chapter 2 - What is Amazon Echo? 12

Chapter 3 - Getting Started with Echo 18

Chapter 4 - Connectivity and Device Settings....................23

Chapter 5 - Smart Things and Echo 31

Chapter 6 - Alexa Skills Kit 40

Chapter 7 - Just Some Funny Things..................................42

Chapter 8 - Playing Audio Books with Echo 44

Chapter 9 – Daily Schedule Help.......................................50

Chapter 10 – Shopping with Your Echo..............................55

Chapter 11 – Getting Your Way Around with Echo 62

Chapter 12 – Do More with Voicecast................................67

Chapter 13 – Manage Your Lists 72

Chapter 14 – Echo for the Smart Sports Fan 77

Conclusion 82

BONUS 85

Introduction

I want to thank you and congratulate you for buying the book, "Amazon Echo User Guide: What to Know about Your Amazon Echo, How to Use It & Get The Most out of Your Echo". You may even be considering buying one and just want details of what the Amazon Echo can do for you. Well, this book has it covered and will also be useful as a guide from that point of view.

I believe that everyone should buy Amazon Echo since I think it offers such good value to potential buyers. I think a great many people would like the Amazon Echo even at the full price. It's a sensible decent audio framework at its base level, and the association with Alexa means that it offers quality. It is exceptionally helpful when you need information quickly as the Echo will provide it. After just a couple of hours of using the Echo, you will probably discover, as I did, that you are as indeed coming to depend on Alexa. In fact, once you start to use it, you will wonder how you ever managed without it.

After only a day with the Echo, it's as of now turn into a routine for me to stroll in the front door and request Alexa to play some of my personal favorite music. That is great, as my front entryway is more than thirty feet from the Echo. I tend to do this without thinking about it, which demonstrates the excellence of the Amazon Echo. It has turned out to be part of my every day activities and perhaps it will become a part of your life too.

This book contains proven steps and strategies on how to effectively and efficiently use this device. It will further explain how you can use this device to have a smarter lifestyle. This book will also give an introduction on what SmartThings are and how will they make your life easier with the use of Amazon Echo. Alexa Skills kit is also discussed so that you have all the information you need. This will not only help you setup the particular features on the device but also convince you to buy it if you haven't already purchased this AWESOME, beautifully designed and easy to use device. Amazon Echo is or could be your ultimate Virtual Companion.

Thanks again for buying this book, I hope you enjoy it! It was written because I am enthused about the efficiency of the Amazon Echo and what better recommendation than that of word of mouth from a user of the Amazon Echo? What's in it for me? Passing on word about what it can offer you to make your whole life easier is enough really. My friends were tired of me enthusing about it, and putting it in book format helps me to spread the word.

Chapter 1 – Who Should Consider Buying an Amazon Echo?

When it comes to new technology, people are usually baffled by it, at least until they see what it can offer them in their lives. I was baffled when confronted with the idea of the Amazon Echo because I didn't know if this would be another gadget that would gather dust rather than get used to its full capacity. But that's part of the wonder of this gadget. Who knows what its full capacity is? With a company as strong as Amazon, working behind the scenes to come up with updates and improvements all the time, I think that the kind of people who can benefit from the Amazon Echo would certainly include:

Business people – For keeping an eye on your appointments, the Amazon Echo is a great gadget that can liaise with your Google diary and let you know in advance what plans you have, so that you are able to schedule your work in a more efficient manner. It's also able to do a lot more than that for you. It can be used for a variety of tasks and using its inquiry mode is really helpful when you want fast answers from websites such as Wikipedia. Need to know something? Just ask your Amazon Echo.

There are also different things that you can do on the Amazon Echo which will really impress you. Need to get to a meeting at 10? Know your route? You can ask for traffic updates and that's pretty useful from a time point of view.

Students – If students or kids within the family unit need help with their homework, Amazon Echo can help considerably and kids don't need to know anything too technical. If they need facts, then the Amazon Echo can help them instantly. Simply by asking the Amazon Echo a question, it has a world full of knowledge available to it that can help them to get facts quickly. There's also another feature which can help them, in that books can be read aloud and that's useful when you want to discuss a project with friends or listen to it in a group with other students and then discuss that project. It makes studying a lot easier to stomach. Impress your kids' friends by asking them over to help with their studies. They will certainly be impressed. The learning of languages is easier as books can be read in many different languages which may help them if this is their field of study.

Travelers – Imagine having a one stop place to go to ask about recommended hotels or places to visit in a given area. Well, Amazon Echo comes up trumps and is able to tell you the kind of restaurants, hotels and even the kind of places you can expect to visit in advance, so that vacation planning has never been as easy. More and more information is being added all of the time, so you can be sure to keep on top of the travel game and know exactly what it is that a set location offers you.

Sports enthusiasts – Too busy to watch the game? Don't know what the results were? Then Amazon Echo will keep you updated.

The cook in the house – Imagine having access to recipes just when you need them. The Amazon Echo is able to do so many things, and thus you may find yourself experimenting with cooking even if this isn't usually your thing.

The music freak – Well, you don't have to actually be a freak to enjoy the links that Amazon Echo has with radio stations and all the music that you can handle in any genre whatsoever. It's so useful and all of your purchases are stored so that you have access to them at any time that you want them. Just say "Play Bob Dylan" and Amazon Echo is intelligent enough to actually be able to discuss which track you would like to listen to. For the classical enthusiast, it's a way of opening up your mind to new types of classical music because when you hear something that you love, but that you don't own, you can always use Amazon Echo to order it. Remember, this is your assistant and as an assistant, the Amazon Echo is happy to help you to increase your knowledge of music and also supply the music that really does hit the spot.

The senior – Listening to audio books is something that can help those who have poor eyesight, but it isn't just the senior that benefits from the use of the Amazon Echo. Anyone who wants to listen to audio books can listen. It's particularly relevant though to seniors if they are finding it hard to read. Imagine being able to switch the Amazon Echo on and off easily and use it just like picking up or putting down a book. That's one handy gadget for those who still need the stimulation of reading material but who can no longer manage to read the small print in a book.

The homeowner – The scene is set, you choose the music and you tell Amazon Echo to dim the lights. Yes, it can. In fact, it's so intelligent that it can do several smart tasks around your home and that's a really cool feature. At the moment, the limitations of this are not enough to put people off because it's all new technology, but imagine a future where you can tell your Amazon Echo to turn on the oven and to set it to a certain temperature. Now that really means that you can cook without too much effort and that's pretty clever isn't it.

The shopaholic – You know when you start to see things that you like, they play on your mind for a while when you go home. I remember feeling this way about a puzzle that I saw a friend had bought and I really wanted one. Amazon Echo took all the frustration out of the picture. I simply asked it to purchase the puzzle and described it and was very happy when it was able to distinguish this from my description and purchase it for me. That's pretty neat stuff and it's all voice activated. Once you have set Amazon Echo up, you are in charge. Say the wake word, and the Amazon Echo is ready to do whatever you tell it to. I wish somehow there was a way that it could take the dog for a walk but perhaps they will come up with exercises for your pets at some stage in the future. For the time being, having the availability to shop in this way is really neat and those who buy frequently on Amazon.com will be happy that it's very simple.

This book is based on what the Amazon Echo can do now, but it's worth bearing in mind that the Amazon Echo is evolving. You can see from this chapter that the Amazon Echo is useful for all kinds of people. Thus, the amount of use that the family will get from it is something worth bearing in mind. As it's a very discreet gadget, setting it up is very simple and it won't take up as much space as that 45 inch TV screen!

All it needs is to be placed somewhere that has access to an electrical outlet and within the range of a Wi Fi connection and you're good to go. Working in conjunction with an app which can be downloaded to your tablet or phone, it couldn't be easier. In fact, setting it all up really doesn't take that much time at all. I thought it would be harder and for someone who is technically challenged, it really didn't need me to understand anything outside of my existing limited scope of knowledge. Thus, I would have no hesitation in recommending it to people whose lives are busy and who want a home personal assistant. Nicknamed "Alexa" the Amazon Echo will really go out of its way to help you without imposing itself upon you and that's a lot more than many gadgets that are too much of an imposition.

In the next chapters, I will walk you through what you can do with the Amazon Echo in more fine detail, so that you can use this book to help make the most of your experience.

Chapter 2 - What is Amazon Echo?

Amazon Echo, otherwise called Alexa, is a voice recognition gadget from Amazon.com with capacities including being able to reply to your inquiries, play music and control smart gadgets. This very small and unimposing gadget comprises a 9.25-inch tall cylindrical speaker with a seven-piece receiver cluster, speakers that incorporate a woofer/tweeter and a remote control. The device reacts to the name "Alexa"; however, this "wake word" can be changed by the client/user (from a given choice of names by Amazon). Amazon has been evolving Echo inside its Lab126 in Silicon Valley and Cambridge, Mass., for no less than four years. The gadget codenamed "Doppler" or 'Task D', was a part of Amazon's first endeavor to extend its gadget portfolio past the first Kindle E-reader and it's certainly done that.

Amazon unleashed a surprising new gadget on the tech world with the Echo, a device that gives away little at first glance. It doesn't look exciting and this belies what you can actually get from it. What is it? Where did it originate from? Do you require one? These are all sensible things that a consumer may ask. Fortunately, we have answers for you in this guide which will also expand your knowledge of the Echo. I wish that someone had explained what the Echo does to me and that's one of the reasons I have written this guide. However, I did learn and must admit that I enjoyed every moment of getting close up and personal with my new best friend.

Amazon Echo works around recognizing your voice and the more you use it, the easier it does it. It is hands-free and is switched on all the time. However, it's not actively doing what you want it to do until you wake it up with the wake word. With seven mouthpieces or very sensitive microphones, and shaft framing innovation, Echo can hear you from all over the room, even while music is playing. It can even hear you if there is talking going on or people present. I tested this while having a dinner party and among the other voices, it was easily able to distinguish my voice which was impressive. This device additionally is an expertly tuned speaker that can fill any room with immersive sound. Amazon Echo associates with Alexa, a cloud-based voice administration, to give data, answer inquiries, play music, read the news, and give climate information or check games scores, and the sky is the limit from there. It's a question of what you want to use it for really. All you need to do is ask. This particular device will start acting when it recognizes the wake word. You can pick Alexa or Amazon as your wake word. These are easy words to remember, so that means that turning it on is very simple indeed.

The Amazon Echo is an appealingly designed speaker, and its voice-control framework can adjust to your living space and has exceptionally good sound quality. The speaker's Wi-Fi setup is generally clear, and you can likewise straightforwardly associate the Echo with through Bluetooth with your smart phone or tablet. Amazon has kept on including helpful elements since the item was initially launched and will continue to do so, which means that your updates keep you completely up to minute as far as innovation goes. If Amazon add something to its capabilities, it is downloaded when an update is done and that means your Amazon Echo is always going to be the latest technology.

It's a Bluetooth speaker

Maybe most importantly, the Amazon Echo is a Bluetooth speaker. That implies you can unite any Bluetooth-proficient gadget - from an iPhone to your tablet - to it wirelessly to play music or other sounds.

All things considered, this small cylindrical chassis has some very interesting components. Amazon calls it "advanced audio design." The inner components of the Echo are mostly comprised of audio parts, like "dual downward firing." These are speakers that let the sound shoot 360 degrees outward and all around the device. That gives wonderful quality of sound which surprised me and delighted me both at the same time.

The Echo comes with a remote control with an implicit built-in microphone and music playback as well as volume controls, and as a Wi-Fi empowered device, it can access music services like Amazon Music, Prime Music, iHeartRadio, and TuneIn, meaning that your access to music is fantastic. You also have the power to turn it down or up by a single voice command. That's useful if you don't happen to like the volume being too high.

Far- Field Voice Recognition

Tucked under the light ring on the Echo are a variety of seven amplifiers/microphones. These sensors utilize "beam-forming technology" to hear you from any direction no matter where you are (hence the name Echo). The microphones within the device and the ones in the remote control are always on and are always listening to you. Don't think of that as a disadvantage because while it's listening, it's working on recognizing your voice in a more comprehensive way.

With upgraded noise cancelation, Echo can hear you pose a question even while it's playing music. It utilizes on-gadget watchword spotting to identify the wake word. At the point when the Echo identifies the wake word, it lights up and streams sound to the cloud, and that's when you can start having fun and use the Echo to answer your questions or to comply with your demands.

It has search functionality

We've already told you that the Amazon Echo has music-providing capacities, and that it's generally on and always hearing you. So what is it listening for?

The answer is a solitary word; "Alexa." Saying "Alexa" where the Echo can hear you is similar to stating "Hey Siri" when your iPhone 6 feels like listening to you. As such, it stands out enough to be noticed.

Also, the primary thing you'll be doing once you have the Echo's attention is looking for music and much, much more. You can instruct it to play a certain singer or tune, yet you can likewise ask general inquiries: "Will it rain tomorrow?" "When is Thanksgiving?" and ask it for "recipes." These are just a few of the examples of its capabilities. The point is that it knows you are addressing it once you have used that magic word "Alexa" and will be ready to either answer you or provide you with what you have asked of it.

The Amazon Echo is more than a gadget. As you will read in the future chapters, it can do so much for you – help you with organization, shopping, provide answers to your questions and be integrated into your home very easily indeed. The Amazon Echo is small enough to be discreet, but don't be fooled by that relatively unimposing exterior. It does a lot of things and it does them efficiently. Even senior members of your family will be able to use it with ease to read their book to them, and the voice is crystal clear which makes it even more enticing as a personal assistant.

Ever-Evolving

Alexa—the mind behind Echo—is inherent in the cloud, so it is continually getting smarter. The more you use Echo, the more it adjusts to your patterns of speech, vocabulary, and individual likes and dislikes. Furthermore, in light of the fact that Echo is constantly connected, it automatically updates all on its own. Amazon are continually adding new abilities to Echo. As of late, they have included getting music from Pandora, book recordings from Audible, Google Calendar access, live games scores and timetables, movement reports, Amazon.com re-requests, Philips Hue, SmartThings, Wink, and the sky really is the limit from here as new things are being added all of the time.

The Echo will eventually have the capacity to control more smart home gadgets. Furthermore, there's dependably a chance it'll adjust to include more services. That is the thing that makes me the most amped up about the Echo. It's an astounding and very clever music player today. However, it additionally has the possibility to develop into the center for everything electronic in a home. Imagine having your coffee made upon request or having the oven switched on when you need it. Although these are not things that you can do now, the advancement of technology brings this kind of functionality closer all the time.

According to what has already been talked about, the Echo can deal with your schedules, alerts and updates, and it can likewise play radio stations, but that doesn't mean that this is the device's limit. The ability to constantly update leads the Echo to learn and improve all the time and that also includes those Echo devices which have already been put into use. The app that you use for all this functionality is very simple to use and you intuitively know what to do just by looking at the options available.

Envision the potential it could have to be connected to your entire house. "Alexa, turn the warmth up in the kitchen;" "Alexa, is the main door locked?" The best part is that this way you wouldn't need to depend on Kinect any longer, and you would certainly feel more in control of your own home. It will be a while before the Amazon Echo gets to let the cat out into the yard, but who knows? Wherever Amazon Echo is leading, you can bet your life that it's innovative and that it won't take you long to adjust to adding new things as and when these become available. "Alexa, dim the lights to 2" is enough for me for now, but there's a lot more to it than that and Amazon are working on updates all the time.

Chapter 3 - Getting Started with Echo

To begin with the Amazon Echo, put your gadget into a central area (no less than eight inches from any dividers and windows). You can put the Amazon Echo into a mixed bag of areas, including your kitchen counter, your main sitting area, your room and a lot of other places as long as you respect the eight inch rule. It is relatively discreet, so it's easy to find a home for it.

Switching on the Echo

Initially, the device needs to be turned on. For this purpose, plug the power connector included in the pack into the Amazon Echo and then into an electrical outlet. The light ring on Amazon Echo turns blue, and later it will turn orange. At the point when the light turns orange, Amazon Echo welcomes you.

Download the Echo App

Download the free application to your tablet or phone. Begin the download process in your phone browser at:

www.amazon.com/echosetup

Opening the application will promptly begin the setup process. While setting up, you will require the Echo to connect to the Internet.

With the free Alexa application for Fire OS, Android, iOS, and bolstered desktop web programs, you can easily manage your music, shopping records, alarms and that's only the tip of the iceberg. The Alexa application is accessible on cell phones with:

o   Fire OS 2.0 or higher
o   Android 4.0 or higher
o   iOS 7.0 or higher

To download the Alexa application, go to the application store on your cell phone and search for "Alexa app," or select a connection beneath:

o   Amazon App store
o   Google Play
o   Apple App Store

You can likewise go to https://alexa.amazon.com from Safari, Chrome, Firefox or Internet Explorer (10 or higher) on your Wi-Fi empowered PC.
*To learn more about the Alexa app, refer to the next chapters.

Connect Amazon Echo to a Wi-Fi network

Follow the detailed guidelines in the app to join Amazon Echo to a Wi-Fi system. For more information, go to **Connect to Wi-Fi**. It should be as straightforward as that, but there is a tip below for those situations where it doesn't recognize your Wi Fi connection.

Tip: If your Amazon Echo doesn't associate with your Wi-Fi system, unplug it and after that connect it to an electrical outlet to restart it. In the event that regardless of restarting it, you experience difficulty, reset your Amazon Echo to its factory settings and set it up once more. To find more detailed instructions, go to **Reset Your Amazon Echo**.

Talk to Amazon Echo

You can now utilize your Amazon Echo. To begin your experience, say the "wake word" and after that talk normally to your Amazon Echo. Your Amazon Echo is set to react to the wake word "Alexa" by default, yet this can be changed to "Amazon" within the app. In the application, go to **Settings**, select your **Amazon Echo**, and afterward select **Wake word**. As previously stated, Amazon Echo uses a special system to recognize what you are saying and will react to the wake word. It then streams sound to the Cloud, including a small amount of sound prior to the wake word having been spoken.

Colors of the ring on Amazon Echo. This gives you an overview of what the Amazon Echo is doing when the different colors are showing.

Spinning cyan color or blue	Echo is starting up
Orange light	Echo is connecting to Wi Fi
Directional light pointing at you	Echo is dealing with your inquiry
Red light	This means that you have deactivated the microphones and need to turn the unit back on again to use it

White light	This happens when you are adjusting the volume

That's not all there is to it though. If there is no light on the Amazon Echo, it means that the Amazon Echo is active, but you have not asked it to do anything or it means that there is an interruption to the power. Check your connection to the wall socket. The other color to look out for is violet as this means that there is a problem connecting to the Wi Fi. These colors help you to get what you want fast.

One of the best things about this color coding is that you can instantly see what the Amazon Echo is doing at a glance and can see if it is responding to your requests.

Remember also that if you have any problem at all during the set up and connection stages, you can refer to Amazon's help page and if you still have problems, their back up team will be pleased to help you. I don't think that you will experience much problem because, as stated, I had very little technical experience and was able to set this up in a matter of minutes and think that most people will have the same experience.

Remember, if you do turn off the microphones at some stage, you need to actually physically press the button on the top of the Amazon Echo to switch them back on again. Your wake word will not do it because you have disabled the microphones and Alexa cannot hear you in this state.

Although there is a volume ring on the top of the Amazon Echo, once your microphones are active, you can adjust the volume with a command instead of using this, if you do not want to get up and use it. That's what's so good about

Amazon Echo. It doesn't demand your attention. In fact, it's the other way around. Amazon Echo is waiting for your commands and will respond very quickly once they are given. Always use the Alexa word so that it recognizes instantly that you are addressing it.

Remember that the remote control is sold separately and if you want access to Alexa from all over your home, you will need this. This can be bought from Amazon and is a real boost to your system because it puts so much within your reach easily even if you are in another room. If, on the other hand, you will always be using Amazon Echo from the room where it is placed, then this is something that isn't strictly necessary and the unit will work without it because of the sensitivity of the microphones.

Talking to the Amazon Echo becomes second nature after a very short time and I found myself asking it silly questions just to see what its capabilities were and was surprised at how cleverly the Amazon Echo deals with all your inquiries and how accurate the translation of your voice is compared with other gadgets of this ilk. Certainly, in comparison with speaking to Google, the hit rate was very high indeed and since it's only your voice that the Amazon Echo is listening to, it soon gets accustomed to your speech habits, although you can make a point of improving your speech anyway as this isn't a bad idea. However, Alexa won't demand that you do and doesn't have a problem with accents like Google apparently does.

Chapter 4 - Connectivity and Device Settings

Amazon Echo provides a varied range of services and each one of these services can be easily enabled on this device by a system which is called "Pairing" or recognizing what new device is being introduced into the equation.

Pairing Mobile Devices

Your Amazon Echo is Bluetooth-empowered so you can stream well-known sound services like Spotify from a cell phone, (for example, your telephone or tablet). Before you can stream sound from your cell phone to the Amazon Echo, you have to pair it with the Amazon Echo so that the Echo recognizes the source that you wish to use. To combine the gadget, verify that it is turned on, set to matching mode (pairing mode), and stay within the range of your Amazon Echo.

Note: Phone calls, instant messages, and different notices from your cell phone can't be received or read by Amazon Echo, and sound from Amazon Echo can't be sent to Bluetooth speakers or earphones. That means that your information is secure at all times.

With your voice

- Say, **"Alexa, pair**." Your Amazon Echo reacts with "Prepared to pair. Go to the Bluetooth settings on your cell phone, and pick 'Echo ###'."

- Open the Bluetooth settings menu on your cell phone, and select your Amazon Echo. It may take a few moments for Amazon Echo to show up in the lineup. Your Amazon Echo will respond with "***Connected with Bluetooth***" once it's successful.

- When you're done utilizing your cell phone, say, "***Alexa, disconnect***." Amazon Echo then disengages from your cell phone.

It really is as simple as that which means that you can pair and disconnect within a matter of seconds. The Bluetooth connection is very stable and you won't find that you have any distortion.

Another way to pair is through the Alexa App

- Open the left route menu, and afterward go to **Settings.**

- Select the name of your Amazon Echo.

- Select **Bluetooth > Pairing Mode**. Your Amazon Echo reacts with "Prepared to pair". Go to the Bluetooth settings on your cell phone, and pick 'Echo-###'."

- Open the Bluetooth settings menu on your cell phone, and select your Amazon Echo. It may take a few moments for Amazon Echo to show up in the lineup. When it's effective, your Amazon Echo reacts with "Joined with Bluetooth."

- When you're done utilizing your cell phone, say, **"Alexa, disconnect**." Amazon Echo then detaches from your cell phone.

After it's matched, your cell phone naturally interfaces with Amazon Echo when you turn on Bluetooth and say, **"Alexa, connect**." If your Amazon Echo is combined with different gadgets, it unites with the latest matched device.

Use Hands-Free Voice Control for Paired Devices

After you connect a cell phone, (for example, a telephone or tablet) with Amazon Echo, you can use its hands free voice control to listen to music, book recordings and more from that gadget on your Amazon Echo. In order to activate this feature, you need to:

- Say, **"*Alexa, connect*."** Your Amazon Echo looks for your cell phone and instantly connects with it.

- Open an application, (for example, Spotify) on your cell phone and select a track to hear it out on your Amazon Echo. You can utilize these voice summons to control playback:

  - Play
  - Pause
  - Previous
  - Next
  - Stop
  - Resume
  - Restart

As you can see these are pretty standard commands which you can easily associate with your music and that makes them very simple to remember and use.

Amazon Echo responds very quickly and the quality of the sound is good. You will find that there is very little distortion and that it's equally as good as listening to music on a hi-fi system and takes up a lot less space. In fact, it's so discreet that it's hard to work out where the sound is coming from, so it won't be like in the old days when you could locate the speakers from the sound. That was always an irritation because it meant that the quality was impaired from various locations within the room. That isn't the case with the Amazon Echo. The quality is consistent and surprisingly good from any location within the room.

Note: If you ask for tunes, collections, craftsmen or playlists, Amazon Echo delays playback on your cell phone and detaches from it. Music from your Amazon Music library plays. To play music over Bluetooth once more, say "*Alexa, connect*" and press play on your mobile.

Pairing Amazon Echo Remote

The Amazon Echo Remote is an optional accessory you can use to identify with your Amazon Echo. Remember only one remote can be paired with Amazon Echo at a time.

Note: The Amazon Echo Remote is sold independently.

To set it up, you need to follow the instructions below.

- Pull down the lock on the remote's battery door, and after that draw the battery door away from the remote. It works in the same way as most TV remotes do so it should be simple enough.

- Insert the two AAA batteries (included) into the remote, and after that put the battery door back on again. Verify the batteries are placed in the right directions before you put the door back on again.

- From the Alexa application, open the left navigation menu, and after that select **Settings**.

- Select your gadget, and after that select **Pair Remote**.

Note: You may see **Forget Remote** in the application. This implies that a remote is now matched with your Amazon Echo. In case, you're supplanting your remote, select **Forget Remote** before you combine another remote with your gadget.

- Amazon Echo searches for your remote and joins with it within a period of 40 seconds. On the off chance that you experience difficulty, press and hold the **Play/Pause** button on the remote for five seconds.

Remember that when you use the remote, you are instantly in control without having to say the wake word. The Amazon Echo listens and reacts to your commands. The neat thing about the control is that you have the usual commands such as volume up and down just as you would on any other remote, just as you can instantly jump from one track to the next at the push of a button instead of asking Amazon Echo to do it through a voice command. You do need to press the "talk" button which is located right next to the microphone if you wish to give instructions to Amazon Echo from the remote.

Microphone

Can the microphone on your Amazon Echo be switched off since its ALWAYS listening? The answer to your question is a simple YES. The microphone on this device can be switched off just by pushing the microphone *on/off* button located on the top of the device. When the light ring the Echo device turns red, it indicates that the microphone is turned off. Amazon Echo won't react to the wake word, nor will it react to the activity catch, until you reactivate the mouthpiece by pushing the microphone **on/off** button once more. Although even if your microphone is off, Amazon Echo will still react to demands you make through your Amazon Echo remote.

Is there an advantage to switching off the microphone?

Actually, I don't believe that there is. Since the system is learning from your voice all the time, you may actually be making it harder for the device to recognize your voice if you always keep it switched off when not using it. You don't have to worry about "Big Brother" listening in either because all the information that it gathers is on the cloud and can be deleted if you really want to delete it. However, it's useful for the Amazon Echo's memory, if you want to call it that, since its recognition of your voice will be enhanced the more you use it.

The microphones are super sensitive and Alexa is listening to increase her understanding of your voice and that's useful to you because it means that responses will become even more efficient than they are now. It's almost as if Alexa gets to know your habits and because of all this recording of your voice is able to pick up on your instructions in seconds because it can anticipate what it is that you are requesting before you have actually finished requesting it and that's pretty smart technology.

Chapter 5 - Smart Things and Echo

It is very exciting to know that SmartThings is now compatible with Amazon Echo which is bound to add more value to the product. This means you can use it for more things. This is great for house security, for lighting, for making sure that doors are locked, etc., and SmartThings are increasing all of the time, which means that Amazon Echo's capacity is increasing all of the time as new gadgets are introduced by Amazon.

What are SmartThings?

SmartThings empowers customers to connect, oversee, and screen their homes by means of their cell phones using the SmartThings portable application for iOS, Android, and Windows Phone. Inside the home, the SmartThings Hub can be combined with a mixed bag of SmartThings' marked sensors and also to third party associated gadgets. The Hub is sold on a stand-alone premise or as a feature of a few starter smart home packs. These packs incorporate mean that the owner is able to use them to automate things within their homes, such as lighting.

SmartThings is a particularly versatile framework to which clients can include many associated gadgets - locks, light switches, outlets, indoor regulators and that's just the beginning—from an assortment of manufacturers. SmartThings is now compatible with numerous gadgets including the Amazon Echo. That gives real power to the homeowner.

Amazon released a software development kit (SDK) for Echo recently which is its smart, voice-controlled speaker. That SDK is similar to an arrangement of plans on the best way to program an outside gadget to work specifically with the Echo - now, the SmartThings associated home framework is hopping on board as well and that's good news from the consumer's point of view.

The amalgamation bodes well for both sides. For Amazon, it helps support Echo's shrewd home credibility and with SmartThings, it makes the Echo a very suitable device for homeowners to use for other things that can help in the security of their homes or smart interaction. Turn the lights down to suit the mood. Make sure that the house is locked and there are a lot more things being added all the time. It's a very worthwhile part of the actions that can be taken by the Amazon Echo making it a very complete virtual assistant to the shrewd homeowner. Thus it's worthwhile getting to know all of its capabilities and embracing the new technology that is happening all of the time.

How to Connect Amazon Echo with SmartThings

SmartThings can associate with Amazon Echo as a Hub Service to give you commands to use in your smart home through mechanized and voice controls. The control of this is very easy as you can see below. I have put this in a step by step manner so that you can easily follow the instructions and get connected quickly.

To begin:

1. Download the **Smart Things** application and create an account.

2. Set up your Amazon Echo and download the Amazon Echo application.

To connect Smart Things with Amazon Echo:

1. In the Amazon Echo application, select *Settings*

2. Select *Connected Home*

3. Under Device Links, select *Link with SmartThings*

4. Enter your SmartThings email and passcode

5. Tap *Log in*

6. Select your *SmartThings Location* in from dropdown menu

7. My device list will populate with your SmartThings on/off and dimmer switches

8. Check the containers alongside the gadgets you need to give Amazon Echo access to

9. Tap *Authorize*

10. You will see this message: "Alexa has been effectively connected with SmartThings."

11. Close the window by tapping *X*

You will come back to Settings. From here, direct Amazon Echo to find the gadgets you have approved access to:

1. Under Devices, select *Discover gadgets*, OR

2. Say, "Alexa, finds new gadgets."

3. The application will demonstrate an advancement bar while Alexa is searching for gadgets

4. Wait for the "search to be complete" message

5. Discovered gadgets will populate under Devices; logged off gadgets will be turned gray

You can then communicate with these joined gadgets utilizing Echo's hands-free voice control. Experiment with these expressions:

"Alexa, turn on/off the room light."

"Alexa set the room light to 10." (Brightness can be changed on a size of 0 - 100.)

It's a good idea to practice with the devices because that also gives Alexa time to get to know your voice which will help it in future to recognize these commands in a quicker fashion. You will also note as you go through the set up what kinds of devices can be added and this may fire up your enthusiasm to keep ahead of the crowd by incorporating smart tools that can be added to your kit. As more and more smart things are added to the list of possibilities, it's worthwhile looking at your app from time to time to see if there are any other changes that you can make to your home, so that they can also be included. Keep your app updated to the latest version so that you are always aware of what can be added.

You never know, that dream of switching on the oven at a set temperature and a set time may not be that far into the future and think about how that would revolutionize your home living! For the moment, there's enough for you to get interested and to get accustomed to how it all works, but as stated, there are more gadgets being added all the time so you keep ahead of the game by making sure that your application is always up to date and is the latest version.

Updating devices through SmartThings

Once associated with Amazon Echo, the SmartThings portable application will permit you to design which gadgets are controllable. Just use the progressions shown below.

You can also use these steps to add another gadget to a current setup. Thus, it's worthwhile keeping this booklet handy so that you know how to do it at any time in the future as your home evolves. Again, these are step by step for ease of use and you will get accustomed to using the app easily as the order remains the same for each addition of a device to the system.

1. In the SmartThings application, tap *My Home*

2. Tap *SmartApps*

3. Tap *Amazon Echo*

4. The "My device" list will list the gadgets Amazon Echo has admittance to

5. Tap *My gadget rundown* to see all your SmartThings switches

6. Check the boxes apart from the gadgets you need to give Amazon Echo access to

7. Tap *Done*

8. Tap *next* and take the in-application Device Discovery directions

9. Tap done once more.

It's fairly straightforward once you have done it and adding more smart technology to your home will enable many more functions to be included. Amazon have certainly thought ahead and it's easier to use than a lot of other gadgets and responds very well indeed to new and innovative technology.

To disconnect SmartThings from Amazon Echo

Uninstalling the Amazon Echo SmartApp inside of SmartThings will totally detach Alexa from your gadgets. Your Amazon Echo will no more acknowledge verbal orders for SmartThings gadgets.

1. In the SmartThings application, tap *My Home*

2. Tap *SmartApps*

3. Tap *Amazon Echo*

4. Tap *Uninstall*

5. Confirm by tapping *Uninstall*

Another way to disconnect SmartThings with Echo is:

1. In the Amazon Echo application, select *Settings*

2. Select *Connected Home*

3. Under Device Links, select *Unlink* from SmartThings

4. Confirm by tapping *Unlink*

The time when this is useful may be when you move home and no longer need control of the devices within your old home. Your needs will change and evolve and thus the way that the Amazon Echo makes it easy to connect and unlink, you will find that your Amazon Echo grows with you and is adaptable to your current lifestyle.

As Amazon Echo updates are done behind the scenes, you won't have to buy another. That's the best thing about the Echo and something that should reassure consumers that they are getting the best value for money that they can, rather than having to replace the Echo when new technology makes it outmoded. It won't happen and the Amazon Echo will continue to evolve and improve using the same base unit that you originally bought.

Chapter 6 - Alexa Skills Kit

Alexa gives you the possibility to do a lot of things. Samples of Alexa activities include the capacity to play music from various suppliers, answer general learning inquiries, and give climate figure data, set an alarm or clock, and make inquiries of Wikipedia, among other things. The Alexa Skills Kit gives you a chance to use Alexa more comprehensively by add new capabilities to Alexa as and when you want to. Clients can access all of these functions simply by asking Alexa when the Echo is switched on. *How Alexa Works*

At the point when a client asks Alexa any inquiry or asks Alexa to do something, that demand is sent to the Alexa administration in the cloud. The Alexa administration figures out what the client is attempting to do and although this may appear to be time consuming, it's actually not. The administration can send back content that Alexa reads out loud to the owner of the Echo. The administration can likewise display graphical cards to clients through the Amazon Alexa App, the partner application accessible for Fire OS, Android, iOS, and desktop web programs.

At the point when planning and building your expertise, your voice is being recorded and will get better recognized as you continue to use the Echo. You additionally make a cloud-based administration that recognizes your commands and keeps records of what you have been requesting. You don't have to do any explaining or characteristic dialect as the Alexa administration deals with that. Note that nothing is introduced on any client gadget – the code you create is conveyed to the cloud, either as an AWS Lambda work (an Amazon Web Services offering) or a web administration that you have control over yourself.

That puts you in control and that's important to Amazon, because they want customers that are satisfied with the services being offered to them.

Chapter 7 - Just Some Funny Things

You can always run out of things to ask Alexa and because of that we have decided to give you a few options. You can ask Alexa any of the following funny things and just have a good laugh. Need some exceptionally cool ideas for getting the most out of your Amazon Echo? You're in the right place and probably at the right time. A few questions that you can ask are as followed:

- What is the loneliest number?

- "Alexa, you want the truth?"

- "Alexa, Who ya gonna call?"

- "Alexa, Are you hungry?"

- "Alexa, Please tell me a joke

Apart from asking these questions; there are other certain cool tricks that you can do with your Amazon Echo. For starters, you can torment your family from another room utilizing the Amazon Echo. All you need is a remote. You can always talk into the remote from another room and have the Echo say fun things to your family. Your family members will believe that Alexa is talking to them.

To make the Echo say whatever you want it to (well, just about), utilize the command "Alexa, Simon says..." trailed by what you need it to say. Lamentably, in the event that you utilize obscenity, it will simply beep. Yes, it has been tried as Amazon knew it would be.

For all the people who are not really that good at math, Alexa can always come in handy. There are step by step instructions to utilize the Amazon Echo for basic math. You can request that Alexa "add up two and four" or "what is two added to four". Echo comprehends coasting point values, so you can likewise ask it "divide 478.55 by 209.67" and it will figure it out really well. Obviously, attempting to motivate Echo to divide by zero doesn't work. Be that as it may, that is not Alexa's shortcoming. I point the finger at Newton.

If you want to try something really funny, wait until your daughter brings her boyfriend home and change the music if you find that they are behaving a little too seriously! There are some really fun tracks out there that can help you with this. You may even find that there are tracks you can use to remind your kids that Alexa is watching them when they are watching TV instead of doing their homework!

Chapter 8 - Playing Audio Books with Echo

Bookworms will love using the Echo to read books. Alexa will be your storyteller as she reads audio book upon audio book to your heart's content. And since Alexa is constantly evolving and is connected to the Cloud at all times, it will be able to search for good reads online so that you can also expand your reading collection. This may be handy if you have an elderly relative who needs company.

Have you ever wanted to read a good book but just could not do it because you simply do not have the time? Now you will be able to read even a few chapters while you are cooking, working out, doing household chores or just lazing around with the help of Alexa.

How do you listen to audiobooks with Alexa?

Alexa is always in touch with the latest reads from Audible and Kindle Unlimited. Audible and Kindle Unlimited are Amazon companies and therefore, getting your audio books from these online stores is easy, fast and very convenient.

To start with Audible

Audible is where you will find more than 180,000 audio titles and the best part is that your first story is absolutely free. Subscription is easy and moreover, you also get to start with a 30-day trial. To be able to listen to Audible audio books from Alexa, you need to create an account first.

The first 30 days are free at Audible and then it costs $14.95 thereafter. After successfully subscribing to Audible, download the free app to your android or smartphone.

To start with Kindle Unlimited

Kindle Unlimited is Amazon's library of thousands of audio books all professionally narrated using Whispersync for Voice. There are so many different genres, fantastic authors and a lot of perks when you start using Kindle Unlimited. Purchasing an Echo comes with a free Kindle Unlimited subscription. Therefore, you get instant access to all the best audio book materials when you use the Echo.

"Alexa read my book."

Once you have your subscriptions ready and you have already synched your device with Echo, you can pick an audio book from your library and ask Alexa to read it for you. You can

- **Listen to a new audio book title**

No more moving through your list of audiobooks. You will never be frustrated in looking for what you need from your library with Alexa, simply say "Alexa, play the book [title]." Alexa will immediately locate the audiobook and read it right from the first page. You can also use other commands such as "Play [title] from Audible" if the book is located in Audible or simply say "Read [title]" and Alexa will instantly recognize that you are referring to an audiobook track.

- **Listen to a book that you were reading a while ago**

Life is so full of interruptions and just when the chapter is getting more and more interesting, you need to do something important! You can ask Alexa to read from where you left off by telling it to "Resume my book" or "Resume [title]" and it will immediately read the sentence, paragraph or page where you left off. That's really good because it means that you don't have to go through the process of skipping forward to get to where you last finished your book.

- **Navigate through the audiobook as if you are turning the pages**

You can ask Alexa to go forward, backward and pause reading by saying simple commands such as "Go back, Go forward" or "Pause." Alexa will understand where you want to go; it will go forward or backward in the audiobook by 30 seconds to find the right page. Thus, if you are a reader that skips over certain sections of a book, you can get Alexa to do this too!

- **Program Alexa to start or stop reading during a particular time**

Turn Alexa into a smart bedtime story reader for your child and even for yourself by setting up a sleep timer. Simply say "Alexa, set a sleep timer for [x] minutes /hours" or "Stop reading the book in [x] minutes/hours." If you want to cancel a sleep timer, you may also tell Alexa to stop by saying "Cancel sleep timer."

- **Ask Alexa to find audiobooks for you through the Cloud**

If you want Alexa to find a new audiobook or you would like to expand your reading genre, simply ask her to find a particular title or to search for a list of books from the author from the Cloud. Alexa will continuously grow her list of audiobooks according to your searches, meaning that you can expand your horizons easily.

Some material that Alexa does not support

Alexa is a smart and ever-growing reading assistant and a wonderful bedtime storyteller but she also has some limitations. It does not support the following content that is available at Audible:

- Newspaper

- Magazine audio subscriptions

- Chapter navigation by voice, stats and badges

- Bookmarks

- Navigation speed

These limitations will not be a hindrance your audiobook enjoyment since you can use the existing features that the Echo has. Developers of the Echo guarantee that Alexa will continuously evolve and may soon cover these limitations so watch this space. However, even though news is not covered by newspaper, you can get the latest scores on your favorite games and also the weather, which is important.

More ways to enjoy reading audiobooks with Alexa

People with disabilities will be able to use Alexa in helping them read various selections from the Cloud. The blind may use Echo to read their favorite audiobooks just like asking a friend to do so.

If you wish to learn a new language, Alexa could help you do so by reading books from that language. You will be amazed as to how the device can pronounce words and even sound just like a natural native speaker!

If you are unsure of any word or you would like to look up the meaning or you would like to access the web for more information about the book and any selection from the book, all you need to do is to ask Alexa to pause and say a command to search or do something.

You can start reading a book from your device such as a smartphone, Android device or Kindle and then pause to do something and resume listening to the book with Alexa. All you need to do is to sync a compatible device or app with the Echo and you will surely be good to go.

Get the whole family and start listening to an audio book together with Alexa. This is great for bedtime reading, or for studying a book together.

Chapter 9 – Daily Schedule Help

Echo is a device that will not just serve you real time information and play music, it will also make your life simpler and a lot more organized. If you have a Google account, you can link your Google Calendar with Alexa to allow the device to read events straight from your calendar and schedule.

In fact, Alexa can also help other members of your family synch their own Google Calendars with Alexa.

Why sync your calendar with Echo?

It is easy to get carried away with a lot of things over the course of a busy day. Not everyone is perfect. You can be too tired to remember to pick up someone, to greet a family member on his birthday or to call a friend regarding an important matter. With the help of your Google Calendar, enter the events on the specific day and time and simply save them. If you are very forgetful and you would want someone to remind you about your schedule, you can use Alexa to help you.

Special note

When you use this feature, you might be revealing your schedule or your reminder for everyone listening to Alexa. You might be playing music or using the service for other features and suddenly it reminds you of a date or a secret engagement! Everyone interacting with Alexa will hear your events so you better be careful! However, if you have no secrets and want to be reminded of your schedule, then it's perfect for this purpose. I have set out below a step by step introduction and you will find that this is easy to follow.

How to set up Echo

- **Linking your Google Calendar**

  - Start by opening the Alexa app in your device

  - Open the left navigation panel in the app

  - Select Settings > Calendar

  - Select Link Google Calendar Account

  - Sign in using your Google email address and enter your password. If you do not have a Google account, create one and then follow the remaining steps.

  - After following all the steps carefully, you will now be able to use this feature.

- **To access information from your calendar, say the following commands:**

  - "Alexa, when is my next event?"

  - "What's on my calendar today?"

  - "What's on my calendar on [specific day or time]?

- **To access information from another person's calendar, you my say the following commands:**

  - "Alexa, what is on John's calendar today?"

  - "What's on Sarah's calendar this afternoon?"

The person's calendar should be synched with Alexa as well.

Additional ways that Alexa could help you with your schedule

Alexa keeps on getting better and better each day. Along with telling you and reminding you what to do for days and weeks, you can ask your device all sorts of information to make your life easier and more organized, as described below.

Going someplace new

If you are scheduled to go on a vacation or a trip but you are anxious about what to take, what to do and any other kind of worry, Alexa could help you find the information you need. For instance, if you are travelling to Hong Kong for the first time, ask Alexa for the best hotels in the area, the most popular food in the city, the most common greetings that people say and even the weather when you travel. Alexa constantly expands its information so you can get the most updated info as well. It's very useful for language tips and if you are all traveling as a family, you can practice your greetings together.

Traffic information

Reminding you about a meeting or a date is easy but what about getting there minus the heavy traffic? Ask Alexa for the quickest route to the venue or ask about the traffic conditions on a particular highway or street. Since Alexa is connected to the Cloud at all times, it will inform you about traffic conditions and the latest news that could help you with your navigation. Get to your date or business meeting fast with the help of Echo.

Order or book your seat ahead of time

As you save events in your calendar, you may also use Echo to help you book ahead of time. You can ask Alexa about the number of the restaurant where your meeting or date will be so you can book a table days before or you can ask Alexa when the next Lakers game is and get information on how to book tickets weeks or days before. You will save a lot of time and of course get your life more organized when you use this handy feature.

The Alexa Flash Briefing

One of the most convenient features that Alexa has is Flash Briefing where the device delivers pre-recorded updates from popular broadcasters as well as the latest news or headlines from The Associated Press and updated information from AccuWeather. You can do this every morning when you wake up, just like a personal assistant telling you what your day will be like today. This is easy to use and something that you are likely to include in your daily routine that will give you an overview of what's happening today.

How to do it

1. From the Alexa app, go to the left navigation panel and then select Settings

2. Choose Flash Briefing

3. Customize your Flash Briefing by indicating which shows, headlines and weather updates you want to hear.

4. Command Alexa by saying "What's my Flash Briefing?" or "What's new?"

Alexa will keep on speaking until she is finished with your Flash Briefing for the day but you can interrupt the device by navigating through the Flash Briefing feature. You can say next, previous or cancel if you wish to exit the feature.

Flash Briefing is an important feature that will help you get more organized especially during the start of your day. It is recommended that upon waking up, ask Alexa to start your Flash Briefing as you prepare for work or school. Follow your briefing with your daily schedule and ask for any other items in your schedule that you may have missed.

And before you sleep in the evening, review your schedule using your Google Calendar as well as the Alexa app. Not only will you become more organized but you will find a lot of time to enjoy the day too when you have a smart system to use like Alexa. It actually makes your planning a lot more efficient and you are likely to forget nothing, meaning that you come over as professional and very organized indeed.

Chapter 10 – Shopping with Your Echo

Ah, the wonders of shopping minus all the hassles with Echo! Now, as soon as you think of something to buy or something that you need, you can ask Alexa to remind you about it or you can tell her to place the order immediately.

Echo is from Amazon and as a proud owner of this smart device, you will be able to ask Alexa to place orders for Prime-eligible physical products or to order music through Amazon. Ordering is easy and is also very convenient since you will simply make a command and Alexa follows without any hesitation.

What you need to start placing orders with Alexa

When you ask Alexa to place an order, the device will order the item through the default payment method that you have in your Amazon account. Take note that all the orders that are made for physical products are eligible for free returns and are covered by Amazon's return policy.

You must have

- A US billing address and payment method

- An annual or 30-day free trial Amazon Prime Membership - especially when you want to order or reorder physical products from Amazon.com.

How to buy music with Alexa

Just by asking Alexa, you can order music from the Digital Music Store. The music that you have purchased will be stored in your Amazon Music Library and these do not count against any set storage limits. You can listen, playback or download this music on all the compatible devices that you own that are registered in your Amazon account. If you are already a Prime member, you may add Prime Music in your music library for free.

All the purchases that you make use a 1-Click payment method from the Amazon's Digital Music store. Use the Alexa app to allow confirmation code for every purchase or disable purchasing as well. Simply open the left navigation panel and select Settings > Voice Purchasing to change your settings when you order music.

Alexa will notify you when the purchase has been done, especially when the item is available at no additional cost with Prime Music.

Start shopping for music with Alexa

- **Buying a song or album** – say "Shop for the song [song name]" or "Shop for the album [album name]"

- **Buying a song by an artist** – say "Shop for songs by [name of artist]" or "Shop for new songs by [name of artist]"

- **Buy a song that is currently playing** – if a song that is currently playing catches your interest and you wish to purchase it now, say "Buy this [song /album]" or "Add this [song /album] to my library."

How to buy physical products with Alexa

Amazon Prime members get all the perks of shopping by voice with Alexa. You can ask Alexa to reorder Prime – eligible items that are found in your shopping history. Once you command Alexa to reorder, it will look for the item and then tell you. You must confirm or cancel the order to complete the transaction.

There are times when there are two similar items that are available for you to order and Alexa tells you about this right away. Alexa offers the second item that is available and when you decline this offer, it will order the first item instead.

Alexa cannot find what you want

When your order is not found in your history or Alexa cannot complete the purchase, you will receive a suggestion straight from Amazon's Choice. The choices available for you are highly-rated and well-priced and are available with Prime shipping.

If this happens, you will receive a response from Alexa which is something like this:

For instance you ordered silk sheets which are not in your order history, Alexa replies: "I didn't find that in your order history but Amazon's Choice for silk sheets is [the item available]. The order total price is $[price]. Should I order it?"

The item you requested is not in Amazon's Choice

If the item you requested is not found in Amazon's Choice, Alexa will inform you and places the item that you requested in your personal shopping list instead.

If you "accidentally" placed the order

For any reason you have accidentally placed an order, or if you have ordered it and you no longer want the item, you can tell Alexa to cancel the order. Say "Alexa, cancel order." You may also do so through the Alexa app or visit Amazon.com to make the cancellation.

More shopping responses from Alexa

Understand the following responses from Alexa, your very own shopping diva:

- **Alexa finds a previous order for the item you requested** – if you have a confirmation code "[Item]. The order total price is $[price]. To order it, tell me your voice code."

- **Alexa cannot find a previous order for the item and it is not available at Amazon's Choice** – "I didn't find that in your past orders, so I've added [item] to your Shopping list."

- **The item you ordered is not available at Amazon Prime** – "I found [item] but can only reorder Prime-eligible products. Check your Alexa app for more options."

- **If the item you requested is out of stock** – "I found [item], but it's temporarily out of stock and should arrive around [date]. The order total is $[price]. Should I order it?"

- **The item is available for Prime shipping but is an Add-on item or a Prime Pantry item** – "I found [item], but can't order Add-on items/ Prime Pantry items. Check your Alexa app for more options."

- **If you requested an item from Amazon without Prime membership** – "I found [item], but can only re-order products for Prime members. Check your Alexa app for more options."

- **If you requested an order but there is a problem with your billing information in Amazon** – "Sorry, but there's a problem with the billing address on your account. Please visit Amazon.com to complete your order."

Alexa is your shopping assistant day in and out. And what's even better than an assistant is that it keeps getting smarter and smarter as it uses the Cloud and your own shopping choices to create the best shopping experience for you.

Does all this functionality cost you any more than simply buying the Amazon Echo?

There is no extra cost. You will need WiFi connection. Whether you become a member of Amazon Prime is your own choice. However, there is no monthly fee for the use of Amazon Echo. Let's face it, it's to everyone's benefit that you use it – Yours from the point of view of convenience, and Amazons because no doubt you will make purchases.

Shopping Tip

Alexa is great at keeping your shopping list, but if you want to add new things to that list, you have to keep using the word Alexa. That can be irritating and you can't simple say "Alexa, add coffee, sugar and milk to my shopping list" as it will only include the coffee. Thus, you need to learn to speak Alexa style so that your shopping list is always updated correctly.

If you are going to use the shopping list feature, it's a good idea to transfer your list into a portable app, if you want to know what's on that physical list because you can't access it from a distance if you can't get an Internet connection in the shops. That's an easy one to work around but your list is actually kept on the cloud, so you do need to have Internet access to see it.

I have pointed out these disadvantages because it's handy to know them in advance. That way, you can prepare for your outdoor shopping in a more organized manner and not be disappointed with Alexa's capabilities. It isn't the Amazon Echo that is failing in these circumstances. It is my own organization and as long as I have Internet Access – and in most stores I do – then there really is no problem. However, if you live in a remote area where connection is difficult, expect to have difficulty accessing your shopping list.

Overall, for purchasing online, the Amazon Echo is great and much of what I purchase is available and can be ordered directly through the Amazon Echo. However, when you need to keep a shopping list, make sure that you can access it when you are out to avoid that frustration.

Chapter 11 – Getting Your Way Around with Echo

Travelers and commuters need to stay smart to be able to get to their destination safely and quickly. Time is very valuable for everyone and therefore Echo has devised a way to keep you abreast with the latest traffic information as well as travelling tips and techniques.

Yes, Alexa will be able to help you with the latest traffic conditions in the metro and providing you with the quickest direction or route to take from your starting point to your destination.

How to start receiving traffic info from Alexa

1) Start setting up from the Alexa app

2) Open the left navigation panel and then access *Settings > Traffic*

3) Enter the address of your starting point. The address should contain the street *name, city, state and ZIP code*. Then add the complete destination address.

4) When you are done, click *Save.*

5) You may also add additional stops in your route. Click on the *New Stop* to do this and then click *Save.*

How to ask Alexa for traffic updates

Now that your device is ready and you have added the

starting point and destination, you may now ask Alexa for advice. You can go about this by asking "How is traffic?" or "What's traffic like right now?"

Alexa will respond with the latest traffic conditions giving the names of the streets, avenues and intersections that you will pass to get to your destination. You may also receive some news alerts should there be any kind of major updates such as a vehicular accident or a road blockage. Use these vital pieces of information so you can plan your day ahead minus all the potential traffic troubles.

Searching for places with Alexa

Aside from telling the traffic conditions in and around your route, Alexa will be able to help you locate different places nearby. Alexa can find these places through the use of Yelp. The device can tell you the nearest local restaurants, shops and a lot of different businesses with respect to your current address and information. Yelp is an online directory where you can find different local places and businesses. It is the site where most online folks check for information when they need to find businesses or restaurants that offer top-rated service and businesses that provide highly recommended service and products too. By partnering with Yelp, Echo becomes smarter and definitely more efficient day after day. Every single day, new businesses are being added in Yelp either locally or in other cities. You will find that using Alexa will make your search for particular places easier and of course more fun. Here is a complete guide on how to go about looking for places with the help of Alexa.

How to start looking for places with Alexa

- Start setting up from the Alexa app

- Open the left navigation panel and then access **Settings**

- Select the device you are using and then click **Edit**

- Enter the address of your starting point. The address should contain the **street name, city, state and ZIP code**

- When you are done, **click Save.**

How to ask Alexa for different places

- **Search for restaurants or different businesses** – "What [businesses/restaurants] are nearby?"

- **Search for top-rated businesses or restaurants** - "What are some top-rated [businesses/restaurants] are nearby?"

- **Searching for address of a nearby business or restaurant** – "Find the address for a nearby [businesses/restaurant]."

- **Searching for the phone number** - "Find the phone number for a nearby [businesses/restaurant]."

- **Searching for the hours of operation** - "Find the hours for a nearby [businesses/restaurant]."

How to use these features altogether

If you frequently commute and you love to travel and go to different places around your city, you will love the convenience that the Echo has to offer. Just like having a friend or a personal assistant to help you manage your day, Alexa will be able to pretty much answer anything that you ask it regarding the different places and road conditions. You just have to make these features work in a way that suits your activity and needs.

Frequently update your Alexa app

If you are planning to take a trip or you wish to eat out with friends next weekend, don't forget to update your Alexa app. Make your days out with friends and family more meaningful by arriving on time and reducing the stress of commuting or driving along the way. Alexa will make travelling faster and more trouble free thus allowing you to spend more quality time with your friends or family members. That's a very valuable asset to have.

Add a destination point as soon as possible

Once you have received news that you need to travel, add the destination point in your app. And as soon as you learn some changes in your plan, update your app as soon as possible too.

Take the Echo with you when you travel

The beauty of using the Echo is that you can take it anywhere you want to go. If you need to stay in a hotel in a foreign city, you can take it and set it up. All it needs is a stable Wi-Fi connection and you are good to go. In this new city, you can ask Alexa to find routes, places to eat, places to check out and venues where you can have fun. Because the Amazon Echo is so small and portable, that means it's easy to find a place for it in your suitcase.

Let the whole family become smart commuters

Educate the family on how to use Alexa and how they could improve their commute time and manage their every day schedule. You will see that every family member will love to use the Echo to help them everywhere they want to go.

Make it a habit to check traffic conditions, road conditions and locations of the places that you will need to go before you leave home with Alexa. This makes you and your family smart commuters through and through! Children will be very fast learners and they will also learn from making this a joint exercise just how much time can be saved if you plan before making any trip. That will save them a lot of frustration when they get old enough to drive themselves or need to get out and about. On the last vacation that we had, instead of packing her dolls as she usually did, our daughter was the first to suggest that we take Alexa as a member of the family that she was so accustomed to talking to that it seemed strange not to take her!

Chapter 12 – Do More with Voicecast

Do you have a lot of devices at hand? Have you often wished you could transfer information seamlessly and easily from one device to another? If you have a Fire tablet you can use a new feature that allows you to do this almost like magic.

Alexa will soon become your convenient, and smart assistant. Another one of its amazing functions is that it can allow you to ask Alexa to send additional information about news, weather and places to your Fire tablet. Alexa also has an Automatic Voicecast so that you can do all these automatically. Your Fire tablet should run on Fire OS 4.5.1 or above to be able to perform this feature.

How Alexa manages Voicecast

Alexa starts to send content to your tablet using Voicecast, a notification will appear on the locked screen of your tablet telling you that the information is ready to be saved on your device. If you are currently using the Fire tablet such as you are playing a game, checking your mail or browsing the web, a simple notification will be seen in the Quick Settings menu of your tablet telling you that Alexa sent some information.

You can use Voicecast with the most popular features of Alexa:

1. **Music** – easily transfer music files from Alexa to your Fire tablet, no need for wires or any other physical connection. You can download or purchase music using Alexa and then share it to your Fire tablet in just one command.

2. **Wikipedia** – ask Alexa anything from Wikipedia and send it to your Fire tablet easily. Alexa will easily search it for you so you won't need to lift a finger to search on your device.

3. **Flash Briefing** – remember Flash Briefing the feature that allows Alexa to brief you the day's news, weather and traffic? You can save and send this information from Alexa to your tablet so you can review these pieces of information while you are on the go.

4. **Questions and Answers** – let Alexa search for a couple or maybe ten questions at a time and send these to your tablet. You can access these some other time or take the tablet with you to school or to the office.

5. **Lists** – you need to take your list elsewhere so tell Alexa to send these to your Fire tablet so you can look at these later. You can update your list, save it in the Cloud and access it later through Alexa. Remember you will have to have an Internet connection to access these lists.

6. **Weather** – following the weather? Are you checking for chances of rain? How about snowfall? Monitor all these through Alexa and then send information to your Fire tablet easily via Voicecast.

7. **Timer and alarms** – no need to set the same alarm or timer in your Fire tablet when you have Alexa and Voicecast. Transfer timer and alarm information to your device so that the two will synch even when you are not at home.

8. **Help** – you can get help from all the features of Alexa and transfer this information to your device. Review these so you can use Alexa easier and more efficiently every day.

How to turn on Voicecast

See how easy it is to transfer precious information from Alexa to your Fire tablet? As long as your tablet is using the latest OS, you will never have to worry about losing information again! And of course, it is easy to configure Alexa and your Fire tablet to work with Voicecast. It is easy as three simple steps:

- Access the Alexa app in your Fire tablet.

- Access the left navigation panel and then select *Settings.*

- Select *Voicecast* and then use the switch to power Voicecast on.

Now that you have Voicecast on, you may now command Alexa to send content to your Fire tablet. You may also select Automatic Voicecast so you can transfer information easily and automatically to your device without having to command Alexa. You can find the Automatic Voicecast setting in the Voicecast menu of your Fire tablet settings.

How to tell Alexa to transfer information to your Fire tablet

Everything is set and all you need to do now is to command Alexa to send information. Here is how you do it:

1. Make a request. Remember that your request has to fall among the supported features of Alexa with regards to Voicecast.

2. After Alexa responds, say "Show this on my Fire tablet" or "Send that to [device name].

3. You will now find the information that you requested on your device on the device's locked screen.

There is no limit to the number of information that you would like to be transferred to your device for as long as these are supported by Voicecast.

How Voicecast and Alexa helps you out

Getting precious information from one device to another is a tedious process. Yes there are wireless transfer methods such as Bluetooth but Voicecast takes this a step easier. Once you have accessed information from Alexa, you can automatically send this to your device in a split second. There is neither need to activate Bluetooth or any kind of wireless signal nor the need to use for wires. Therefore, Voicecast makes it a lot easier and more convenient in accessing information day by day.

If you do a lot of research in your career then let Alexa help you out. Easily search for Wiki entries through Wikipedia or ask Alexa any kind of question and then copy these to your device. It saves you time and effort, giving you more time to do other more important things.

Just like having your own personal researcher

Alexa will do all the research so you can review and weigh in on the facts later. You can have the news and weather searched and then read them later in your Fire tablet. There is nothing like fresh, updated and useful information and you can get all these delivered straight to your device.

Chapter 13 – Manage Your Lists

Create shopping lists, to-do lists or New Year's resolution lists in just one command with Alexa. This smart device allows you to create 100 items on each list with each item consisting of 256 characters.

If you are the type that easily forgets things or you would want to become more organized, then you could use Echo for a more organized and more efficient day to day life. You can access different lists anytime of the day and update these lists. Label your lists so that Alexa can save entries as you go along. You may even print your lists or check them out in your computer, laptop or on your tablet too.

Access your Shopping List as well as your To-do lists using the Alexa app on your device. This way, you will also be able to review your shopping list on Amazon and manage items easily.

How to command Alexa to access or edit your list

Alexa can do multiple things at once and even while it is playing a song or searching for an answer to a question you just asked, you can command it to access your list or any list that you have. Simply say the following commands:

- **How to add something on your list** – command Alexa "Add [item] to my Shopping List" or "Put [task] on my To-do list."

- **Review the contents of your list** – command Alexa "What's on my Shopping List?" or "What's on my To-do List?"

Access or edit your list through the Alexa app

Alexa is smart and will follow your command, it will keep your list updated and will let you know if your list is due. However, there are times you want to list down a few items in your list that are confidential in nature; the best way to do this is to use the Alexa app on your device instead. How do you access and update a list on the app?

- **Access a list** - select the Shopping List or To-do List from the left navigation panel. You may be able to view your Shopping and To-do List even without connecting to the web using the Alexa app through your tablet or device.

- **Adding an item on your list** – select the Shopping List or To-do List in the left navigation panel. A text field section, input the item that you wish to add and then click on the + sign.

- **Editing your list** – access the list that you wish to change and then type to edit it. When you are done, simply click on Save and your list will be updated.

- **Removing an item from your list** – access the list that you with to edit and then select the downward-facing arrow next to the item that you want to remove. Select Delete item to remove. If you want to delete more items, mark the checkbox located near the item and then click on Delete. If you wish to delete everything on your list, select View selected and then click on the Delete all.

- **Completing a list** – access the list that you have completed. Select the checkbox that is located next to an item. If you wish to view completed lists, select the View completed to do so.

- **Printing a list** – access the Alexa app from your computer or laptop that is connected to a printer and select Print.

Access or edit your list through the Amazon website

You may also edit or view your shopping list through the Amazon website. Users may find this more convenient since they could easily purchase or delete an item on the list. Accessing your Shopping List through Amazon will also allow you to check the different deals and offers on the site.

- **Access a list** – access the Alexa Shopping list from your Amazon homepage.

- **Adding an item on your list** – select the *Shopping List* and in the text field, enter the item that you want to add and then choose *Add to Shopping List.*

- **Editing your list** – access the list that you wish to change hover the cursor on the item that you wish to change and then select *Edit*. Type over the entry to edit. When you are done, select *Save.*

- **Removing an item from your list** – access the list that you wish to edit and then select a checkbox located near the item. Select *Delete Selected*. If you wish to delete all the items on the list, select *Select All* and then *Delete Selected.*

- **Completing a list** – access the list that you have completed. Mark a checkbox that is next to the item and then Mark *Selected Complete*. If you wish to view the list that you have completed, select the View completed.

- **Printing your list** – access your Shopping List from the Amazon website from your computer or laptop that is connected to a printer and select Print.

Why use the Alexa List function

Basically, creating a list or any kind of list is the best way to get more organized. If you want to start being more organized and more efficient next year or next week, you better start thinking about ways to become more organized and Alexa certainly fits the bill!

The convenience of Alexa is that you can simply command using your voice if you wish to create a list, edit, review or complete a list. You do not need a pen, a piece of paper or your device to make a list and what's great is that you can transfer your list to your tablet or device easily too.

I find that use of Alexa takes all the strain out of life because I got into the habit of adding things to lists which then make my life much simpler. It may seem a little strange at first, but when you get used to using it, it becomes second nature.

And using this list to become more productive every day is easy. Once you have added an item on your shopping list or your to-do list, you can review them at the end of the day and make things happen. Technically, a list would become useless if you do not take action in completing it at all.

If you are going to make lists, be aware that you need cloud access to get at those lists and that's important when you are using lists away from home. As long as you have Internet access, you can access your lists. That means that at work or in a public WiFi area, you will always have access to that information and that makes it pretty easy to use to enhance your life and make things a whole lot easier.

Chapter 14 – Echo for the Smart Sports Fan

Are you a basketball fan or do you follow the Formula 1 races? Do you want to check out Roger Federer's stats or do you want to search for the play schedules for the next MLB season? The good news is that Alexa is capable of providing you with the most updated sports news, schedules and scores using its feature called Sports Update.

With Sports Update, you can command Alexa to give you the latest scores and information on upcoming games of your favorite teams in the NBA, MLB, MLS, NHL and the NCAA.

Here are the features of Sports Update that will truly make you the most amazing sports fan of all:

- With Sports Update, you can add up to 15 sports teams coming from across sports leagues. You must select the sports team from the Alexa app to start following your team using Alexa.

- Alexa can also check for the latest stats and scores so you can be updated no matter what you are doing.

- Alexa will also be able to tell you the latest sports news from the news agency that you trust. You can also program Alexa to include sports updates and news in your Flash Briefing.

- Alexa will provide you with the latest info about your favorite sports team even when you are listening to music or the radio. It can hear you even from across the room while the speakers are blaring.

- Alexa is easy to command, all you need is to say "Give me my Sports Update" and it will immediately tell you everything that you need to know.

How to start using Sports Update with Alexa

It is easy to start using Alexa to update you with your favorite sports team. You must first configure this feature using the Alexa app on your device.

- Start the Alexa app on your device. You may also open the Alexa app from a desktop PC or a laptop.

- Access the left navigation panel and then select Settings > Sports Update

- On the field provided type in the name of the sports team that you wish to follow. You will notice that as you type in the sports team, there are some suggestions from the app. You may continue typing or simply choose the suggestions that the app is giving.

- Choose more sports teams to add to your Sports Update.

- When you are done, click on Save.

- You can use the Alexa app to make changes or to edit your choice.

Cheer for your favorite team with Alexa

Now there are sports fans and there is a sports fan with Alexa. With this device you will never be able to miss out on any kind of event or game season after season. But of course, there are a lot of things to do in a day other than worrying about your team or the game. Now you can do a lot of things and be productive as well, while Alexa updates you with the stats and scores.

And together with all the other features that Alexa has, you will surely become the smartest sports fan alive!

1. Use Sports Updates to get the latest schedules of your team. Add these schedules to your calendar and then let Alexa remind you when it happens so you can watch it on television.

2. Use Alexa to find the safest and the quickest route from your home to the stadium where a live game is being held. You use Sports Update to find out when your favorite team is in town.

3. Create a Shopping list of the different team merchandise that you wish to purchase and buy it from Amazon Prime shopping. Remember the Los Angeles Lakers Kobe Bryant replica basketball jersey that you bought last year? Why not reorder this for the coming season using Alexa at Amazon.com? Use Sports Update to find out when the Lakers are playing at the Staples Center soon so you can your friends could watch.

4. If this is the first time you have ordered a product, say a new Nike running shoe, Alexa will recognize this and find the item for you at Amazon Prime. You will be reminded that this is so and tells you to order the product online via Amazon.com.

5. Ask Alexa through Sports Update to check on your favorite player's stats. Compare this with other players in history by asking Alexa about wiki entries. She can tell you the record assists in a final game or the MVP on a particular season; transfer this information to your Fire tablet and wow your friends later

Alexa expands its memory and capabilities season after season

There is no doubt that Alexa becomes better and better season after season. As one game season starts and ends, Alexa adds all this information and retrieves these when you need them. The device accesses information from the Cloud and therefore it has access to all the latest information and sports updates 24 hours a day, 7 days a week

If you want to change the sports team that you are following or a family member would like to add another team, you may all do these through the Alexa app. Simply change the preferred team settings and check if it is in the drop down menu.

So is another heart-stopping season ending at the NBA or is a new spectacular season is next at the MLB? Don't worry; let Alexa be your guide for these great sporting events with Sports Update.

Alexa limitations

Sorry to tennis, mixed martial arts and motorsports fans, at the moment, Alexa is unable to support updates from these. But as mentioned, Alexa is constantly evolving; it won't be long soon when the device will be able to support all kinds of sports even international sporting federations. You may instead use Alexa's ability to search for information in the Cloud and ask for the latest news updates and stats through an ordinary Q and A.

As stated previously, Alexa is updating all of the time and no doubt will include more as time passes. For the time being, you will have to be content with what is being offered, but that's a whole lot!

Conclusion

Thank you again for purchasing this book!

I hope this book was able to help you to figure out the little problems that you were facing or you might face if we have convinced you enough to buy the incredible Amazon Echo.

The next step is to simply follow these guides to initially bring Alexa to life and then update more apps to make your life easier and happier.

Finally, if you enjoyed this book, then I'd like to ask you for a favor, would you be kind enough to leave a review for this book on Amazon? It'd be greatly appreciated!

If you have anything to share about this book, I would highly appreciate if you could leave a review on amazon.com.

Reverberation will enhance after some time, giving you access to new components and approaches to finish things. Utilize the Echo App to directly send criticism to the developers or feel free to email them at Echo-feedback@amazon.com.

Thank you and good luck!

Hello, Again!

We hope you enjoyed this book! If you haven't already, please accept our invitation to join our Special VIP Book Club at tiny.cc/echo-bonus. You won't want to miss these one-of-a-kind book deals and values!

Make sure to sign up right away - this membership gives you access to great e-book deals! You'll discover amazing values and special VIP deals on a huge variety of books in many different topics and niches - just step into our vast library and take your pick!

As we said at the beginning of the book, your FREE Membership entitles you to many amazing benefits:

1. A Wealth of Free Reading Samples

2. Notifications about Free and Discounted Books

3. Special Early-Bird Alerts About New Titles

4. Bonus Video Content

5. Members-Only Reading Guides

6. Special Reports

7. *and even more* FREE Bonuses!

Thanks for reading this book all the way to the end! We hope you enjoyed reading it as much as we did creating it! As promised, here is a link to your FREE Special Bonus content. tiny.cc/echo-bonus Enjoy this gift as our special "thank you" for purchasing this book - we value your interest in our books!

So, thank you for reading, and stay in touch! Don't wait another minute to get your membership –

Visit tiny.cc/echo-bonus to sign up for our Special VIP Book Club TODAY. IT only takes a minute, and you'll get so much special content - and so great deals!

Thank you for your patronage - and happy reading!

BONUS

Thank you for visiting the end of this book.

As your bonus, I have a two extra chapters for you. You will receive another free video after signing up to our Book Club at tiny.cc/echo-bonus

Have fun with your bonus:

Alexa and Other Devices, Apps and Sites

Alexa is a device that works with you and together with other devices, apps and websites and this is through the IFTTT. The IFTTT is a third party service that regulates how different devices, apps and websites work with each other under required protocols or rules. These rules are known as "recipes" and Alexa can use a recipe when you activate it through the app. Once a recipe has been activated, you can interact with Alexa to use them. To explain how this works in real situations, here are some examples:

- **Alexa plus websites**

  You ask "What's in my shopping list?" Alexa responds by telling you the contents of your Shopping List and then

- **Alexa and apps**

  Completing a task is a momentous event for you and Alexa tweets this to your followers on your Twitter account.

- **Alexa and Google**

  You ask Alexa "Give me my Sports Update" so you can check the schedule of the next game. Alexa posts a reminder on you Google Calendar so you will be reminded.

"Cooking with Alexa"

You can create new and exciting recipes with Alexa or you may choose existing ones from all the IFTTT users online. It could take Alexa around 15 minutes to complete a recipe so be patient!

IFTTT will also allow you to set up reminders and actions after you have completed a recipe. At present, Alexa is not yet programmed to be the action of a recipe. For instance: you cannot set Alexa to tell you if there are new posts in your Twitter but instead it just posts on Twitter for you.

How to start Alexa on IFTT

As always, you need to set up Alexa so it could work with IFTT. It takes a few minutes but the results would definitely be amazing!

- If you do not have an IFTT account, create one at https://ifttt.com/join. After you have finished creating an account, follow the next steps to activate IFTT with Alexa.

- Sign in to your IFTT account and then select Activate.

- Visit your Amazon account and then link this with your IFTT account. You can now use Alexa to work with IFTT.

The Amazon Alexa Channel

There are so many recipes that you could try out and you can find them at **https://ifttt.com/amazon_alexa** . You may also look for juicy recipes from other sites online as well as from Alexa dedicated sites and social media sites. Here are a few ones to try out:

- **Add your Alexa To-Dos to Evernote** – as you create dozens upon dozens of To-Do lists with Alexa, you can send them to Evernote. Evernote is a digital workspace where you can collect inspirational ideas, work with tools that you need to become more organized across all the devices you have and even use professional tools to help you become more productive. Alexa becomes your personal assistant and instantly delivers results of your to –dos in Evernote even without being told.

- **Add your Alexa Shopping List to Evernote** – you can become more organized from Alexa down to all the devices that you own using Evernote. Command Alexa to add or edit items in your shopping list and it gets added to your Evernote.

- **Alexa sends shopping list to your Gmail** – large shopping lists such as procuring materials for your business or tackling a large volume Christmas shopping order is made easier by telling Alexa what to include in your list and then sending this list to your Gmail account. Easily edit your list from your email and then send quotes or information to your partners or clients anywhere you may be.

- **Tweet music that you are listening with Alexa** – tweet to your followers about a new song that you are listing to. Tell them to listen with you or to purchase the album. You and your Twitter pals will never be disconnected with Alexa and IFTT.

- **Add your To–do List in Alexa to Todoist** – You can create new lists from Alexa and then get started on these lists at Todoist. This is an app that lets you manage lists and tasks, work on projects and get things done easier. You can use Todoist in school, at work, at home and even on the road. Todoist provides a clean and seamless place where you can work and a lot of features that will let you become more organized such as sharing and collaboration, notifications and so on. Todoist is free so you can let every member of the family to use it together with Alexa.

- **Turn on your television with Alexa and Harmony** – use Alexa as a remote control by telling it to power on, change channels and control volume with Harmony. Harmony is from Logitech. It is a smart remote control app that allows users to create personalized one-touch activities and control different electronic devices such as home entertainment systems, lights, security systems, thermostats, sensors and so much more. So aside from turning on you TV, you can tell Alexa to regulate most of your electronic devices in your home with Harmony.

- **Control Philips Hue lights with Alexa** – tell Alexa to turn on or off and change the hue of your Hue lights in your home using a smart app. Alexa will turn on light switches for you as long as these light are Hue which is a brand of fantastic, electronic lighting that is used in homes, offices and in businesses.

- **Locate a lost phone with Alexa** – Alexa will help you find a lost phone at home. Misplacing your phone at home will become a thing of the past; just tell Alexa to find your phone and it will contact your device and make it ring. You can therefore find your phone easily as long as it is nearby.

- **Alexa connects with wireless HP Printers** - no longer will you need to access your shopping list from a desktop or a laptop so you can print it. Alexa will print your list by connecting with a wireless HP printer.

As you can see, there's a whole lot more to Alexa than you may have first thought when you unwrapped that seemingly small item that is the Amazon Echo. It's more than just a speaker. It's more than just a small piece of technology because the backing that it has from Amazon and the number of different technologies that it supports is amazing. Thus, don't underestimate what you can do with it. You may need to read over the details again as and when you introduce new things to your Amazon Echo experience, but it will be well worthwhile and you will then be getting the best that you can from the initial purchase that you made. That's real value for money.

More Great Stuff

Alexa is expanding its features. There is no doubt that you will be able to use Alexa for more features and enjoy it more. There are currently more great stuff to check out with Alexa so be sure to take note of these:

Controlling more connected home devices

There are currently a handful of devices that you use at home that are supported by Alexa but soon there will be more. Being able to connect these with Alexa makes your home more efficient and in one way, safe and sound for all family members.

You can now use Alexa to power on Insteon, Wink, SmartThings, WeMo and Hue. And possibly this feature is perfect for people that may have mobility issues or someone that may have physical disabilities.

Old people may use Alexa to control their lights and their devices at home since they usually have trouble moving about with their age and condition. People with chronic illnesses and those that are visually impaired may also connect their devices with Alexa so that they could seamlessly control their home environment as well. They may also enjoy the access to music and audio books as these are a real comfort to people living alone and who want to hear a human voice.

Some Alexa commands for controlling home devices are the following:

- "Alexa, discover my devices."

- "Alexa, dim the dining room to 20%"

- "Alexa, turn on the kitchen exhaust fan"

- "Alexa, turn on the patio lights"

Remember that once you connect home devices with Alexa, you and other people may use Echo to operate these devices. You can operate by voice and ask Alexa to control your home devices even if you are listening to music or listening to an audiobook. Echo has a number of microphones plus has a noise cancellation feature that lets you control Alexa even from across the room.

Safety information for using connected home devices

There are a few important things that you should remember when you connect home devices with Alexa.

- Anyone speaking to Alexa will be able to operate the devices and products that are connected to it. This includes devices and products that are used to provide safety and security in your home such as locks and garage doors. Be sure to take extra action to secure your home.

- Follow all the recommendations and instructions when you connect your home device with Alexa. Overlooking a step could cause your safety and security at home to be impaired.

- Take extra action to check the device after you have

made a request. For instance, you requested Alexa to turn off the exhaust fan in your kitchen, after the command, check that it has been done.

- Take extra action to make sure that only you or your members of your household can operate Alexa. You can do this by stopping Alexa from responding to commands by turning off the microphone from the supported device. You may also do this by visiting the Alexa app.

Here are some home devices that support Alexa

Alexa currently controls a number of devices and brands. If you want to create a more automated home and would like to increase the value of your home in the future, invest in devices that support Echo. The following devices are compatible:

Lighting brightness control

Be sure to purchase devices made by Wink, SmartThings, Insteon and Philips Hue. Soon, more and more devices will be supporting Alexa with this technology becoming more and more efficient and more widely used.

Hubs

Take note that some connected home devices will ask you to link a hub device to Alexa before these may be controlled. Devices from Wink, Insteon and SmartThings are one of them. There are hubs that control home devices as well but these are not directly compatible with Alexa. You may be able to control some of these devices but these may provide limited functions and may have poor performance as a result.

How to connect to a hub

Before you connect, visit the app store on your mobile device and download the manufacturer's app for the home device that you wish to connect. Set up and connect the hub as well as any compatible-connected devices to the same Wi-Fi connection as your Echo. Make sure that you have downloaded and installed the latest software updates on your device before you begin.

8. Access the Alexa app and select Settings

9. Choose Connected Home

10. Look for Device Links and select Link with [Service]. A third –party log in will appear. Sign in using your third party information and complete the set up.

11. Add the connected device into your Alexa app.

12. You are now ready to use Alexa to operate these devices.

A connected home device group

Create a group so you can easily control all the devices in a group using very simple, straightforward commands such as "Turn on the patio lights" or "Set the bedroom lights to 30%." Take note that any device groups that you will create in the third –party app will be seen as an individual device in the Alexa app.

- Access the Alexa app and select Settings > Connected

Home.

- Select Groups and Create Group.

- Create a name for the devices in the group. Select a recognizable name preferably with two syllables so that Alexa could easily identify what you mean for instance, you can name all the devices in the bedroom as "Bedroom" or devices that you have connected in the living room as "Living Room." But then again, why not be more creative and designate "Suzy's Room" for your bedroom?

- Select the connected home devices that you want to add to the group you have just created and then click Add.

- You can edit the devices that are included in a group by selecting Groups to select the device group and then edit.

- You can delete the group if you wish by selecting Delete.

Listen to your favorite tunes at Pandora

Another cool feature available for Echo users is listening to Pandora. If you have an existing Pandora account, you can link it using the Alexa app. You will be able to listen to all the custom radio stations that you have saved on your Pandora account. Listen to radio music according to your favorite artist, comedian, track or genre in just one command. Alexa will even help you personalize your music listening pleasure by rating the music that you are currently listening to.

Just say thumbs-up or thumbs-down if you like or dislike the songs. Alexa will remember these and will make your listening more enjoyable as well. You can create new stations using the Alexa device and these will reflect on your Pandora account.

Pandora has a wide selection of radio stations online and when it comes to genre, you can pick from a bevy of music genres from rock to classical music. And possibly what's great about it is that it is free to use. If you do not have a Pandora account yet, you can set up a free account at the official Pandora website.

Setting multiple timers and alarms with Alexa

Do you need to set up three or more timers in succession? Do you want to wake up family members in different times of the day? Alexa can get you going with these through its Timers and Alarms feature.

Special note: each device that is connected with Alexa is independent from other device timers and alarms. You can set up an alarm or timer feature up to 24 hours ahead. Even if your device is muted, the timer feature will still go off. The Alexa app will be able to help you change the timer or alarm volume for each connected device.

Configuring alarms

- **Setting an alarm** - command Alexa to "Wake me up at [time]" or "Set an alarm for [time]." You may also say "Set an alarm for [amount of time] from now."

- **Snooze an alarm** – command Alexa by saying

"Snooze" while you can still hear the alarm. This will snooze the alarm for nine minutes.

- **Find out the status of your alarms** – ask Alexa to provide you the status of your current alarms by commanding "What time is my alarm set for?" If you have multiple alarms set for the day, Alexa will recite each one of them and then tell you to check them using the Alexa app.

- **Stopping an alarm** – say "Stop the alarm" while the alarm is sounding. You can say "Cancel alarm for [time]" and Alexa will stop the alarm for that time but will not delete it. Reset the alarm using the app; it will not automatically set the alarm for you.

  From the app, select Alarm from the left navigation panel and then cancel the alarm that you wish to cancel by selecting Off.

- **Deleting an alarm** – you cannot do this by commanding Alexa; you need to do this via the Alexa app.

  From the app, select Alarm from the left navigation panel and then select the alarm that you wish to remove and select Delete alarm.

- **Changing the alarm volume** – you cannot command Alexa to do this for you. Access Alarm from the left navigation panel and then select the device and then Sounds. Adjust the volume bar from the Alarm and Timer Volume.

Configuring timers

- **Setting a countdown timer** – command Alexa to "Set a timer for [amount of time]" or "Set timer for [time]." A countdown timer may be set for up to 24 hours.

- **Pausing or resuming countdown timer** – you cannot do this with Alexa, you need to use the app to pause or resume timer. Select the Timer from the left navigation panel and then select Edit next to the timer that you wish to pause and click on Pause.

- **Ask Alexa to check for the remaining amount of time** – ask Alexa "How much time is left on my timer?" You may also view the remaining amount of time in your timer through the Alexa app.

- **Stop a countdown timer** – tell Alexa to "Stop the timer" as soon as you hear the timer sound off.

  You may also say "Cancel the timer for [amount of time]" or for an upcoming timer. You may also do this using the Alexa app. There are times when two timers are set for the same amount of time, you need to use the app to cancel which timer you want to cancel or delete completely.

- **Manage timer volume** – you cannot command Alexa to change the timer volume for you. You need to access the Alexa app by selecting Settings from the left navigation panel, select the device you wish to manage and then select Sounds.

Increase or decrease the timer volume by dragging the Alarm and Timer Volume bar.

What if you do not need Alexa?

Some people love to use Alexa for almost everything that they do at home. They love to control the temperature, lighting and security with Alexa; they can't wait for news and sports updates with Alexa and creating and updating lists with the device too. But sometimes, creating an automated life could take the fun out of many things and may even complicate safety and security.

Alexa is ever evolving but you can cancel some of the skills that it has too. Opening or enabling skills are easy; you simply visit the Alexa app, select Skills from the left navigation panel and then enable the skills that you wish to activate.

If you wish to disable some of the skills that Alexa has, simply click Disable and you are good to go.

Developing Alexa

There are Alexa Skills Kits available for Alexa so you can improve its speech processing capabilities to create voice interactive skills. Currently, developers from StubHub, Pebblebee and Glympse are building new skills for Alexa. It won't be long when you can have access to these amazing new skills that will surely enhance the way you use your Echo.

Another free video and many more bonuses are waiting for you.

http://tiny.cc/echo-bonus

Made in the USA
Lexington, KY
21 March 2016